I'VE GOT ME AND I'M GLAD

Rev. Ed.

by
Cherrie Farnette
Imogene Forte
Barbara Loss

Incentive Publications, Inc.
Nashville, Tennessee

Cover & illustrations by Janet Levine March
Edited by Sally Sharpe

ISBN 0-86530-069-0

Table of Contents

LOOKING TO THE FUTURE

PREFACE

I'VE GOT ME AND I'M GLAD is made up of reproducible student activity pages designed to help young people identify their strengths and weaknesses, examine personal preferences, and look to the future. The development of a positive self-concept based on the uniqueness of individual talents, abilities and personality traits is encouraged within the framework of realistic self-appraisal.

Exploration of daily schedules, short and long-range goals, habits, hobbies, successes and failures should extend self-awareness and promote understanding of self and others. Awareness of the interdependence of people who work and/or play together and the multifaceted influences people have on each other are interwoven throughout the experiences. In developing the activities, attention has been given to the individual's role as a citizen, a family member and a participant through aesthetic and recreational experiences.

The high interest/low vocabulary format has been maintained to encourage use of basic communication skills in the most positive and meaningful sense. The simple, easy-to-follow directions are self-explanatory and are designed to encourage student independence and divergent thinking.

Each of the activities is designed to stand alone and to present one complete self-awareness experience. The activities may be used to supplement and reinforce adopted textbooks and courses of study and may be used in either individual or group settings. Although there is no need for a rigid sequence, each teacher will want to review the entire collection and plan the order and manner of presentation to meet the needs of individual students.

* Answers for all pages labeled "*Answer Key" may be found on page 79.

Use words or pictures to describe yourself.
Add something to each section of the mirror to "reflect" your true personality.

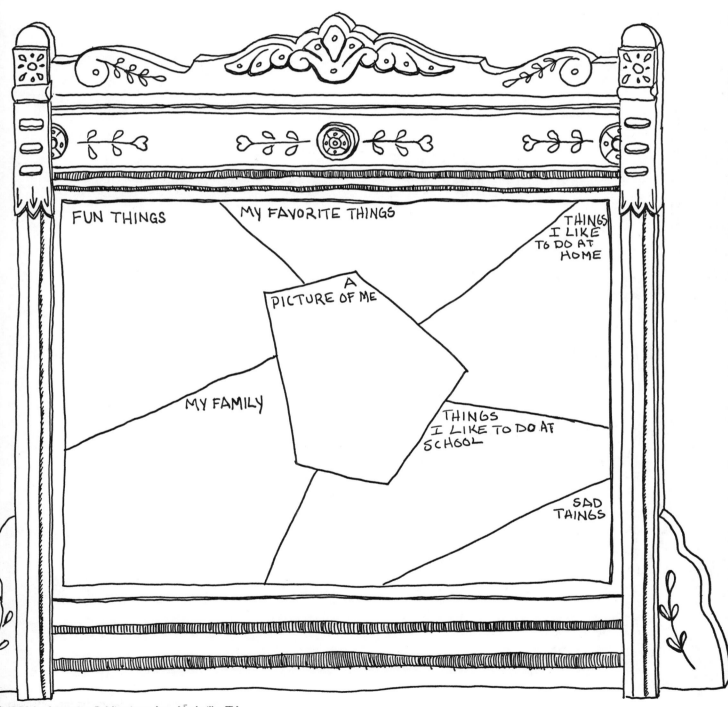

SELF-PORTRAIT

Describe yourself in words and pictures.
Be specific so that others will see you as you see yourself.

WORD PORTRAIT

Describe yourself for someone of your age who has never met you. Help that person to know "the real you" through your words. Include descriptions of your physical characteristics, hobbies, family, school life, favorite sports, social activities, and the other things that are most important to you.

Date _____

Dear Pen Pal,

_____

_____

_____

_____

_____

_____

_____

_____

_____

_____

_____

Sincerely,

_____

BUILDING BLOCKS

Think carefully about your personality and the words that describe the real you.
Then write a word that describes you in each of the boxes below.
Use each word in a sentence to tell why that word describes you.

Follow the notes of the self scale.
Write a sentence for each note's subject.

DO   Something I can do well

_____

RE   member - a most memorable moment

_____

ME   aningful - something very meaningful to me

_____

EL   vorite - my favorite thing

_____

SO   lo - something I do myself

_____

LA   ughter - something that makes me laugh

_____

TI   me - the best time of my day

_____

DO   uble - something I do with someone else

_____

ROUTINE ROUNDUP

Make a schedule of what you do during the day.
Start with the time you wake up and end with the time you go to sleep.

6:00 a.m. _____	2:00 p.m. _____
6:30 a.m. _____	2:30 p.m. _____
7:00 a.m. _____	3:00 p.m. _____
7:30 a.m. _____	3:30 p.m. _____
8:00 a.m. _____	4:00 p.m. _____
8:30 a.m. _____	4:30 p.m. _____
9:00 a.m. _____	5:00 p.m. _____
9:30 a.m. _____	5:30 p.m. _____
10:00 a.m. _____	6:00 p.m. _____
10:30 a.m. _____	6:30 p.m. _____
11:00 a.m. _____	7:00 p.m. _____
11:30 a.m. _____	7:30 p.m. _____
12:00 noon _____	8:00 p.m. _____
12:30 p.m. _____	8:30 p.m. _____
1:00 p.m. _____	9:00 p.m. _____
1:30 p.m. _____	9:30 p.m. _____
	10:00 p.m. _____

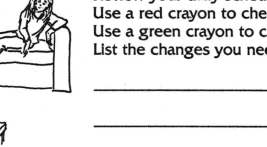

Review your daily schedule.
Use a red crayon to check your three most productive times.
Use a green crayon to check your three least productive times.
List the changes you need to make in your daily schedule.

_____

_____

_____

Complete this newspaper article describing something good you've accomplished today. Include a headline for your article and a "picture" of you and your success.

The Daily Sun

YOUR HOME TOWN   VOL. 1

LOCAL NEWS

Headline:

Today _____ did a very special thing.
(your name)

PERCEPTO GRAPH

Rate yourself on the "percepto graph" below.
Try to be honest!

	Never	Some-times	Most of the time	Always
I finish what I start.				
I am interested in people.				
I am willing to help when I can.				
I try to do what I say I will do.				
I am a loyal friend.				
I feel good about my schoolwork.				
I always want to do a little bit better.				
I try to look my best.				
I am a dependable person.				
I make good decisions.				
I am not easily discouraged.				
I am a good family member.				
I can organize my time.				
I share in completing daily chores.				
I share with others.				
I am easy to get along with.				
Friends like to be with me.				
I am a good sport.				
I talk to others easily.				
I listen to others.				
I follow directions.				
I am able to take criticism.				

Check your "percepto graph" rating and write a few sentences describing
your strong and weak points.

_____

_____

_____

GETTING TO KNOW ME

Complete each statement below to help you examine your feelings and get to know yourself a little better.

Three things I like to do are:

_____

_____

_____

Three things I don't like to do are:

_____

_____

_____

Two things I'd like to see are:

_____

_____

Two things I'd like to hear are:

_____

_____

The school subject I like most is _____ .

The school subject I like least is _____ .

I like to read about _____ .

I daydream about _____ .

If I weren't me, I'd like to be _____ .

It makes me angry when _____ .

I am frightened when _____ .

I need to practice _____ .

Time goes by fastest when I _____ .

Times goes by slowest when I _____ .

I wish that I could _____ .

HELP!

Make a list of things that are the most difficult for you to do and a list
   things that are the easiest for you to do.
After making the lists, identify helpers to assist you with the "difficu
   items.
Make a list of friends that *you* can help.

Difficult	Helper	Easy	Person I Can Help

Think of one very special thing you would like to be able to learn to c
Make a list of three places where you can go for help.

1. _____

2. _____

3. _____

learn more about yourself, write one or two-word answers for the
questions below.

What kind of party do you enjoy most?

_____

Would you rather spend a Saturday at a natural wildlife museum or
an art museum?

_____

Would you rather visit a circus or a zoo?

_____

What kind of movie do you enjoy most?

_____

Which musical instrument do you like most?

_____

If you had your choice of any sporting event, what kind of event
would you attend?

_____

What ride would you select first at an amusement park?

_____

What is your favorite kind of book?

_____

t three things you enjoy doing in your free time.
t a check in the correct column after each item.

OUTDOORS		INDOORS	
with others	by myself	with others	by myself

_____

_____

_____

RATING REACTIONS

UPSET

SAD

OK

HAPPY

DELIGHTED

Rate how you might feel if someone said these things to you.
Select the frog that best describes your reaction and write the number rating in the space provided.
Then write a sentence to explain why you might feel that way.

RATING

1. "That's a nice job. Your score is 100%!" _____

_____

2. "Don't ask questions! Just do what you are told." _____

_____

3. "I don't understand. Will you help me?" _____

_____

4. "I can't ride bikes with you today. Maybe we can do it tomorrow." _____

_____

5. "I can't play with you, so go away. I'm busy." _____

_____

6. "This paper is a mess. Why are you so sloppy?" _____

_____

7. "Copy this paper again. I know you are proud of your work when it is neat." _____

_____

Feeling "OK" means feeling good about yourself and the things you do.
To solve the puzzle and find the hidden word, read the sentences below and color the spaces
as directed.

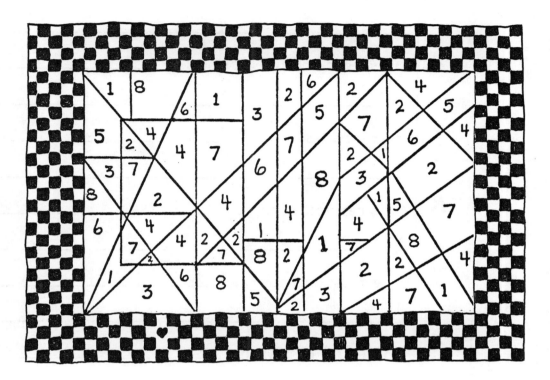

1. If getting praise for something you do makes you feel "OK," color the #1 spaces.

2. If getting punished for something you did not do makes you feel "OK," color the #2 spaces.

3. If doing your best makes you feel "OK," color the #3 spaces.

4. If breaking promises makes you feel "OK," color the #4 spaces.

5. If having friends makes you feel "OK," color the #5 spaces.

6. If making your parents happy makes you feel "OK," color the #6 spaces.

7. If not helping your friends when they need you makes you feel "OK," color the #7 spaces.

8. If being honest makes you feel "OK," color the #8 spaces.

*Answer Key

LOOKING BACK

Complete each sentence below.
Describe times when you might have felt like this.

1. Everyone was looking at me when _____

_____

2. I was most embarrassed when _____

_____

3. I was proudest when _____

_____

4. I was happiest when _____

_____

5. I was most unhappy when _____

_____

6. I looked my best when _____

_____

7. I was scared when _____

_____

8. I had the most fun when _____

_____

EMOTIONAL CROSSWORDS

Complete this crossword puzzle by writing answers in the numbered spaces.

Words To Use:
jeer
sob
angry
cry
scared
enjoy
grin
eager
nice
good
envy
ok
awe
sorry
tired
shy
emotions
glad
mood
gloomy

Across
1. to have a pleasant time
3. exhausted
5. smile
6. all right
7. respect
9. afraid
12. dark and dreary
15. weep
16. sorrowful
17. not bad or poor

Down
1. feelings
2. to make fun of
4. anxious
5. happy
8. jealousy
10. enraged
11. pleasant
13. a state of mind or feeling
14. bashful
16. cry

Select five words in the puzzle and write a sentence for each describing a time when you felt that way.

1. _____

2. _____

3. _____

4. _____

5. _____

© 1989 by Incentive Publications, Inc., Nashville, TN.

*Answer Key

TOUCHING TIMES

Answer these questions about what you do when you have "touchir times."

1. What do you usually do when you are lonely?

_____

What other things could you do?

_____

2. What do you usually do when you are angry?

_____

What other things could you do?

_____

3. What do you usually do when you are anxious or nervous?

_____

What other things could you do?

_____

4. What do you usually do when you are embarrassed?

_____

What other things could you do?

_____

PRINCIPAL

Write a brief paragraph about a time when you were lonely, angry, anxio and/or embarrassed.

_____

_____

_____

_____

Complete this chart by writing specific words in the happy and sad columns below.

TOPIC	Makes Me Happy	Makes Me Sad
Color		
Weather		
Places		
Clothes		
People		
Food		
T.V. Shows		
Books		
Time		
Chores		
Friend		
School Subjects		

SEEING IS NOT ALWAYS BELIEVING

Finish each statement below.

1. Sometimes I look **HAPPY** when I really feel unhappy
because _____ .

For example, when I _____

_____ .

2. Sometimes I look **LIKE I DON'T CARE** when I really do because

_____ .

For example, when I _____

_____ .

3. Sometimes I look **ANGRY** when I'm not because

_____ .

For example, when I _____

_____ .

4. Sometimes I look **SURPRISED** when I'm really not
because _____ .

For example, when I _____

_____ .

5. Sometimes I look **KNOWLEDGEABLE** when, in fact, I am
not because _____ .

For example, when I _____

_____ .

Turn one of the statements around and write your reason.

Example: Sometimes I look unhappy when I really feel happy because . . .

_____

_____

EMOTIONAL NOTIONS

Define each of these words in terms of what it means to you.

Love is: _____

_____

Happiness is: _____

_____

Security is: _____

_____

Friendship is: _____

_____

Beauty is: _____

_____

Trust is: _____

_____

Fame is: _____

_____

Success is: _____

_____

Tolerance is: _____

_____

Communication is: _____

_____

FINDING FEELINGS

Find and circle the words listed below that describe feelings.
Words may be found horizontally, vertically and diagonally, but not
backwards.

```
C S L M A H U R T G N E M
R C G O O D A N G R Y A E
E A N L A L E P O P M G A
A R D N A T T O P M I E N
T E S Z R D A R E Y S R X
I D Y A N Y O A S T E L I
V P M H N U M E A V I A O
E S U N S U C C E S S F U
V R U T R I L L E A N R S
S F R A N K C B T A D A R
U N E E D E D O Y X D I S
M W R S U R P R I S E D G
S C A L M P D E X C I T E
H E R U C E S D L U C K Y
Y A D E R E J E C T E D O
S A D E L I G H T E D E N
```

Feeling Words To Find

afraid	angry	rejected	clever	funny
surprised	upset	good	successful	sad
scared	shy	creative	glad	lucky
mean	smart	anxious	delighted	happy
needed	excited	bored	eager	nice
	hurt		calm	

Using six of the feeling words, write a brief paragraph describing how you feel now.

_____

_____

_____

*Answer Key

efly describe what could happen in each situation given in this negative action chain.

get angry and hit a friend . . .

_____

_____

ignore someone who needs a friend . . .

_____

_____

complain a lot . . .

_____

_____

refuse to take turns . . .

_____

_____

don't do my chores . . .

_____

_____

refuse help from the teacher . . .

_____

_____

refuse to do my part in group activities . . .

_____

_____

ake a list of three other actions that would probably cause negative results.

● _____

● _____

● _____

TEMPER-ATURE

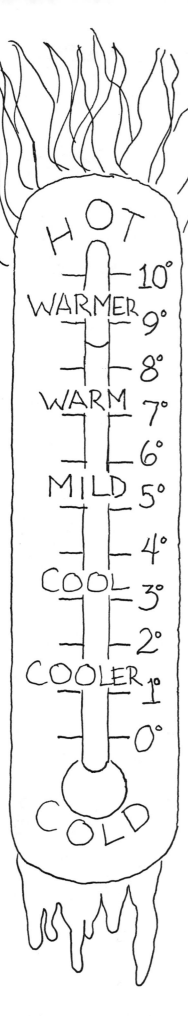

Answer each question below by circling the answer that most nearly describes what you think you would do.

1. You lose your lunch money. Would you:
   a. cry?
   b. borrow some money from a friend?
   c. go without lunch?

2. You are late to school. Would you:
   a. blame someone else?
   b. kick the door?
   c. apologize and explain what happened?

3. You drop your homework in the mud. Would you:
   a. try to find time to copy it?
   b. leave it in the mud?
   c. throw it at a friend?

4. The other team wins. Would you:
   a. stomp away because you think the game was unfair?
   b. shout at your teammates for "blowing" the game?
   c. congratulate the other team?

5. You want to go out but have to stay in and complete your chores. Would you:
   a. grumble and complete them?
   b. complete them but decide to plan ahead next time?
   c. refuse to do them?

To find your "temper-ature," use the rating list below.
Add the points you scored for each answer.
Shade in the total on the thermometer to discover your temper rating.

1. a = 2	b = 0	c = 1
2. a = 1	b = 2	c = 0
3. a = 0	b = 1	c = 2
4. a = 1	b = 2	c = 0
5. a = 1	b = 0	c = 2

Solve these problems.
Describe what you would do if you were faced with each of these situations.

1. You are invited to two birthday parties on the same day.
Your solution:

_____

_____

2. You told your mother you would stay home and play with your little
brother, but your best friend just gave you a ticket to a baseball
game.
Your solution:

_____

_____

3. You borrowed your friend's favorite record and broke it, but you
don't have any money to buy another one.
Your solution:

_____

_____

4. You forgot to do your homework for tomorrow and it is past your
bedtime.
Your solution:

_____

_____

5. You never seem to be able to get up in the morning and you're often
late to school.
Your solution:

_____

_____

6. Your best friend has three tickets to a movie and invites two other
people (but not you) to go along.
Your solution:

_____

_____

MEMORABLE MOMENTS

Write a "memorable moment" in your life for each of the topics below. Briefly describe why each was memorable.

1. Memorable holiday: _____

_____

_____

2. Memorable trip: _____

_____

_____

3. Memorable friends: _____

_____

_____

4. Memorable visitor: _____

_____

_____

5. Memorable party: _____

_____

_____

6. Memorable achievements: _____

_____

_____

Write three sentences to tell about a memorable school day.

_____

_____

_____

DECISIONS, DECISIONS!

In column 1, list three situations in which you had to make a decision today.
In column 2, describe each decision.
In column 3, give the reason for your decision.
In column 4, tell whether or not you think you made the right decision and
    explain your answer.

1 Situation	2 Decision Made	3 Reason	4 Evaluation

Think ahead about a decision you might need to make tomorrow.
Write a brief paragraph about how you think you can best handle the
    decision.

_____

_____

_____

_____

_____

_____

IDEAL LIVING PLAN

Follow these steps to plan your "ideal" room.

1. Think about what you want to do in your room.
2. Complete the planning charts below by listing the things you will need to make your room ideal.
3. Draw your ideal floor plan.

ACTIVITIES PLANNED FOR MY ROOM:

FURNITURE NEEDED:

ACCESSORIES I NEED:

(pillows, curtains, pictures, plants, etc.)

My Ideal Room Floor Plan

POCKETFUL OF CHANGE

Use your magic "change power" to complete each statement.

- If I could change my appearance, I would _____
  _____ .

- If I could change my grade average, I would _____
  _____ .

- If I could change my neighborhood, I would _____
  _____ .

- If I could change my transportation to school, I would _____
  _____ .

- If I could change my bedroom, I would _____
  _____ .

- If I could change my wardrobe, I would _____
  _____ .

- If I could change the subjects I study in school, I would _____
  _____ .

- If I could change the school's physical education program, I would
  _____ .

- If I could change my talents, I would _____
  _____ .

- If I could change my weekends, I would _____
  _____ .

st three other things you would change if you could.

_____

_____

_____

CHANGING THINGS

Imagine that you have the power to make changes in yourself, your home, your school and your world.
List the changes you would make in each of the following areas:

1. Changes In My Home

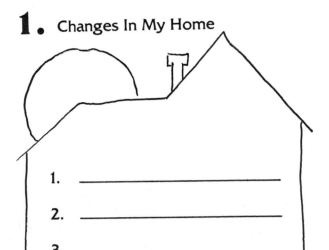

1. _____
2. _____
3. _____

2. Changes In My School

1. _____
2. _____
3. _____

3. Changes In Myself

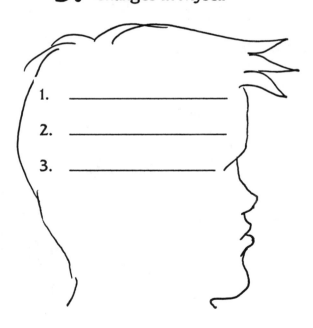

1. _____
2. _____
3. _____

4. Changes In The World

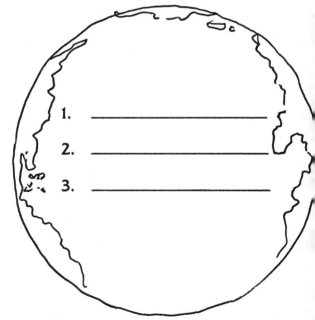

1. _____
2. _____
3. _____

List things that you would not change.

1. _____
2. _____
3. _____
4. _____

IF I COULD

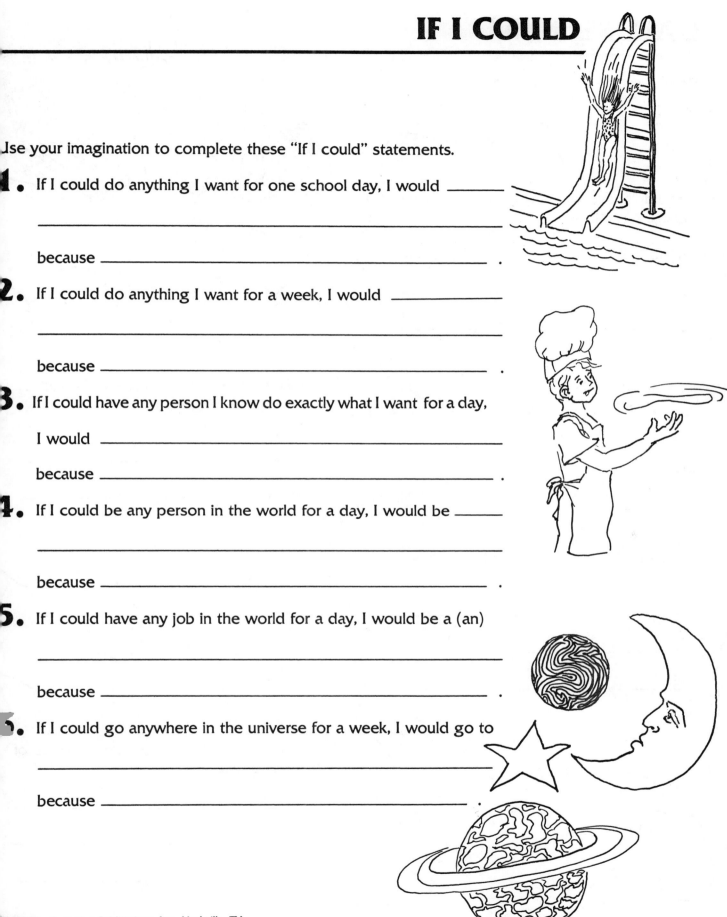

Use your imagination to complete these "If I could" statements.

1. If I could do anything I want for one school day, I would _____
_____

because _____ .

2. If I could do anything I want for a week, I would _____
_____

because _____ .

3. If I could have any person I know do exactly what I want for a day,

I would _____

because _____ .

4. If I could be any person in the world for a day, I would be _____
_____

because _____ .

5. If I could have any job in the world for a day, I would be a (an)
_____

because _____ .

6. If I could go anywhere in the universe for a week, I would go to
_____

because _____ .

DAYDREAMING

Complete the statements below.

If I didn't have to clean my room or do my chores, I could . . .

1. _____
2. _____
3. _____

If I didn't have to go to school, I could . . .

1. _____
2. _____
3. _____

If I didn't have to do my homework, I could . . .

1. _____
2. _____
3. _____

List three other daydream activities of your choice.

1. _____
2. _____
3. _____

LOOK AND FEEL

You can discover clues about how other people feel by looking at them carefully.
Describe how each of these persons might feel.
Write about a time when you felt like the person in each picture.

How does this person feel?

_____

_____

When have you felt this way?

_____

_____

How does this person feel?

_____

_____

When have you felt this way?

_____

_____

How does this person feel?

_____

_____

When have you felt this way?

_____

_____

How does this person feel?

_____

_____

When have you felt this way?

_____

_____

POSITIVE PURCHASES

You have a "word allowance" of $2.50.
Use this allowance to buy words describing the people below.
Then complete the sentences.
Do not spend all of your money on one person!

NICE WORDS

NICE WORD - COST	NICE WORD - COST	NICE WORD - COST
BEAUTIFUL 20¢	SINCERE 15¢	SUCCESSFUL 15¢
FRIENDLY 15¢	DEPENDABLE 25¢	CREATIVE 20¢
HONEST 25¢	INTELLIGENT 20¢	UNDERSTANDING 25¢
GENEROUS 25¢	CAREFUL 15¢	SENSITIVE 20¢
PLEASANT 15¢	POLITE 20¢	HAPPY 20¢
HELPFUL 20¢	THOUGHTFUL 25¢	CHARMING 15¢
FUN 25¢	HUMOROUS 25¢	INTERESTING 20¢
	TALENTED 25¢	

1. My friend is _____

because _____ .

"Nice Words" cost = $ _____

2. My parents are _____

because _____ .

"Nice Words" cost = $ _____

3. My favorite teacher is _____

because _____ .

"Nice Words" cost = $ _____

4. My class is _____

because _____ .

"Nice Words" cost = $ _____

Spend $1.00 to buy "Nice Words" that describe you.
Use these words in a sentence to describe yourself as you would like others to see you.

_____

_____

Write your best "friendly advice" for each situation below.

YOUR PRESCRIPTION

Your friend is upset because she failed an exam.

YOUR PRESCRIPTION

Your friend tells you, between sobs, that his puppy has run away.

YOUR PRESCRIPTION

Your friend just told you he can't go camping with you because he got into trouble at home.

YOUR PRESCRIPTION

Your friend tells you how sad she is because she's sick and cannot go to the class picnic.

YOUR PRESCRIPTION

Your friend tells you he can't find his library book and doesn't know what to do.

YOUR PRESCRIPTION

Your friend tells you with tears in her eyes that she has lost the watch she borrowed from you.

SENSIBLE SOLUTIONS

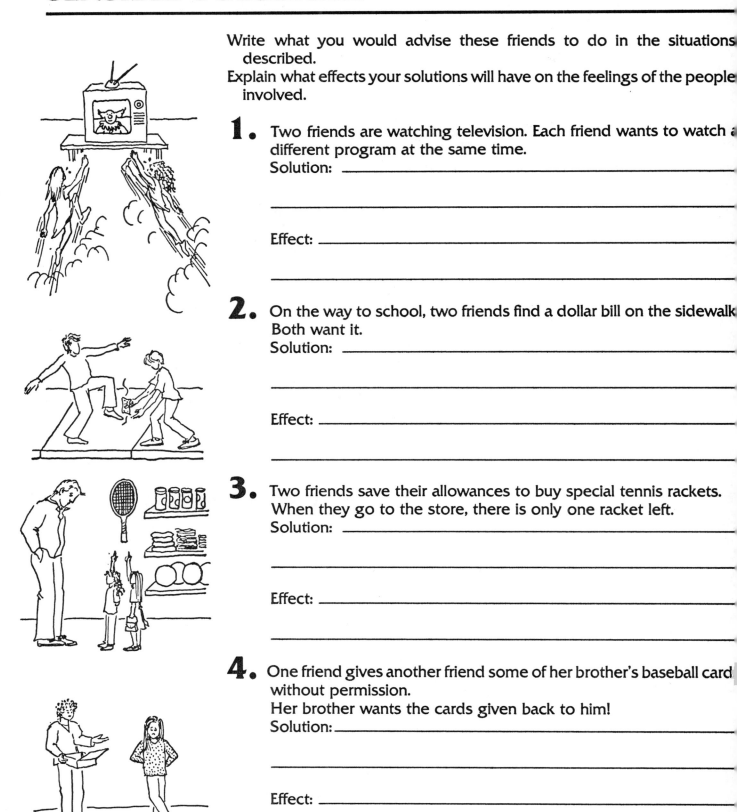

Write what you would advise these friends to do in the situations described.

Explain what effects your solutions will have on the feelings of the people involved.

1. Two friends are watching television. Each friend wants to watch a different program at the same time.

Solution: _____

_____

Effect: _____

_____

2. On the way to school, two friends find a dollar bill on the sidewalk. Both want it.

Solution: _____

_____

Effect: _____

_____

3. Two friends save their allowances to buy special tennis rackets. When they go to the store, there is only one racket left.

Solution: _____

_____

Effect: _____

_____

4. One friend gives another friend some of her brother's baseball cards without permission. Her brother wants the cards given back to him!

Solution: _____

_____

Effect: _____

_____

Award these trophies to the people you feel deserve them.
Inscribe the winners' names on the trophies and list the reasons you have selected each person.

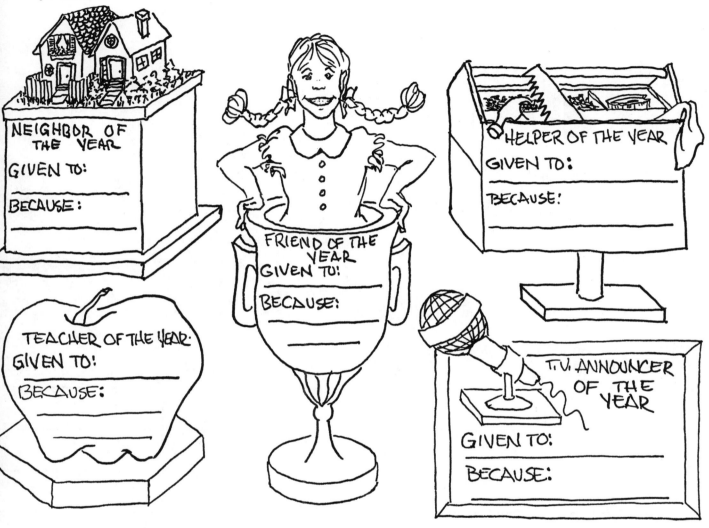

NEIGHBOR OF THE YEAR
GIVEN TO:
BECAUSE:

TEACHER OF THE YEAR:
GIVEN TO:
BECAUSE:

FRIEND OF THE YEAR
GIVEN TO:
BECAUSE:

HELPER OF THE YEAR
GIVEN TO:
BECAUSE:

T.V. ANNOUNCER OF THE YEAR
GIVEN TO:
BECAUSE:

Imagine that you have been selected as "student of the week."
Draw a picture of the trophy you would like to receive.

GETTING TO KNOW YOU

Learn more about your classmates' interests and goals by interviewing ten friends.
Ask the questions on the chart below and record your friends' answers in the correct spaces.

Names of Classmates Interviewed	What is your favorite leisure time activity?	What is your favorite school subject?	What career do you hope to have when you finish school?	Where do you hope to live in ten years?	If you could choose one of these life goals, which would you choose? a. Happiness b. Fame c. W...
1.					
2.					
3.					
4.					
5.					
6.					
7.					
8.					
9.					
10.					

Addy the advisor gives advice to people who have problems with friends.
Assist Addy by reading the letters and writing responses that you feel will help solve the problems.

Dear Addy,

I have a problem and I don't know why. I just can't seem to make friends. I am the smartest, best-looking, nicest, most interesting person I've ever met. Whenever I meet someone, I tell them how terrific I am. They always walk away. What's wrong? Don't they believe me?

I.M. Best

Dear I. M. Best,

_____

_____

_____

_____

Addy's Assistant,

_____
(your name)

Dear Addy,

On the playground, everyone seems to have someone to play with except me. I stand alone by the fence and watch my classmates play, but no one ever asks me to join them. At the lunch table I sit quietly waiting for someone to talk to me, but they never do. I want to have friends. Can you tell me how much longer I should wait for someone to come to me?

R. Shy

Dear R. Shy,

_____

_____

_____

_____

Addy's Assistant,

_____
(your name)

Write a letter to Addy about a problem you are having with a friend.
Ask a classmate to solve your problem by writing a response.

Dear Addy,

_____

_____

_____

_____

_____

IN DIRECTORY

Complete the directory boxes by writing names of people you might contact to get the
  information needed for each situation.
You may have more than one contact person for each situation.

Situations   Contact Persons

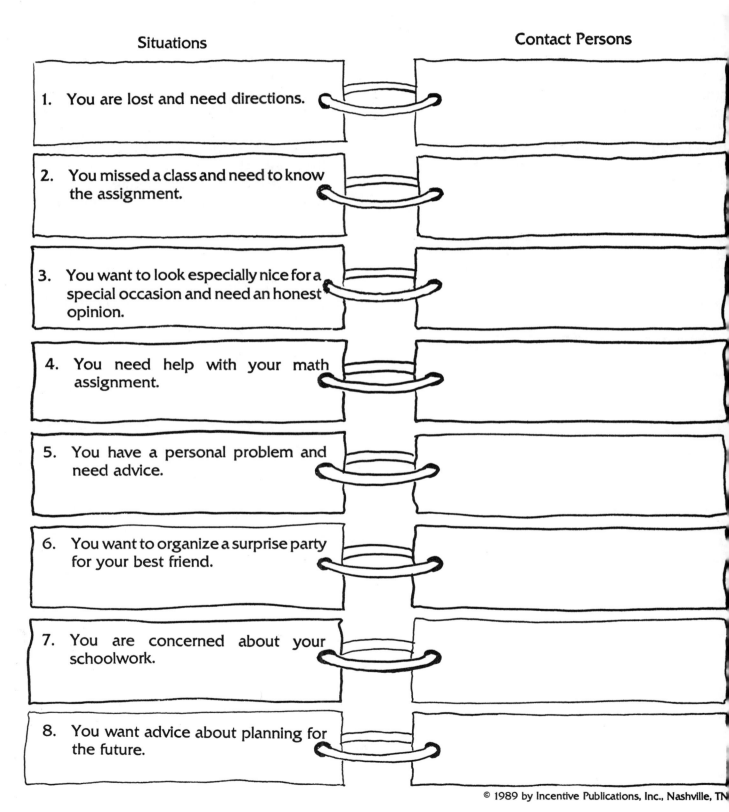

1. You are lost and need directions.

2. You missed a class and need to know the assignment.

3. You want to look especially nice for a special occasion and need an honest opinion.

4. You need help with your math assignment.

5. You have a personal problem and need advice.

6. You want to organize a surprise party for your best friend.

7. You are concerned about your schoolwork.

8. You want advice about planning for the future.

Read each situation and answer the questions.

1. Your class has planned a party. The classmate in charge of refreshments forgot to ask anyone to bring the drinks.

How will this affect the group? _____

_____

How could this situation be avoided in the future? _____

_____

2. Your friends planned to play a game that requires four players. One of the players did not come.

How will this affect the group's plans? _____

_____

How could this situation be avoided in the future? _____

_____

3. Your school project is due. One of the group members didn't complete his assignment.

How will this affect the group? _____

_____

How could this situation be avoided in the future? _____

_____

AFFECTIVE ACTIONS

PROUD
PLEASED

Someone made me feel this way when

_____
_____ .

I made someone feel this way when I

_____
_____ .

Describe a time when someone made you feel like the person in each picture and a time when you made someone else feel that way.

Someone made me feel this way when

_____
_____ .

I made someone feel this way when I

_____
_____ .

ANGRY

SAD
UNHAPPY

Someone made me feel this way when

_____
_____ .

I made someone feel this way when I

_____
_____ .

Someone made me feel this way when

_____
_____ .

I made someone feel this way when I

_____
_____ .

DELIGHTED
HAPPY

POSITIVE CHAINS

Briefly describe what could happen in each situation in this positive action chain.

If I introduce myself to the new student . . .

_____

_____

If I write a letter to a friend . . .

_____

_____

If I offer to help with the paper drive . . .

_____

_____

If I call a friend . . .

_____

_____

If I help with the dishes . . .

_____

_____

If I teach a friend how to play a game . . .

_____

_____

Make a list of three other actions that would probably lead to positive reactions.

1. _____

2. _____

3. _____

DEPENDABLE DAN

Read this story about a typical morning in the life of Dan D. Pendable and answer the questions below.

Dan D. Pendable woke up bright and early. He let his dog go outside and then he fed his fish. Then he woke up his sister. Dan got dressed quickly, combed his hair, brushed his teeth, and rushed outside to feed his dog.

Dan's mother made breakfast for him and packed his lunch. While driving Dan to school, his father reminded him about baseball practice. Dan said, "I couldn't forget that! The team depends on me. I promise you, Dad, that I'll mow the lawn after practice."

"I know you will, Dan," his father said, "because you are a very dependable Pendable!"

1. What things did Dan do that make him dependable?

_____

_____

2. Who depends on Dan? _____

_____

3. On whom does Dan depend? _____

_____

List three "dependable" things that you do almost every day.

1. _____

2. _____

3. _____

MOODY DESCRIPTIONS

Match the titles to the illustrations below.

Write the correct title and a description of the "mood" illustrated beside each picture.

"On Top of the World"
"Dog Tired"
"Higher Than a Kite"
"In a Bind"
"Crabby"
"In the Dumps"

Title _____

Description _____

_____

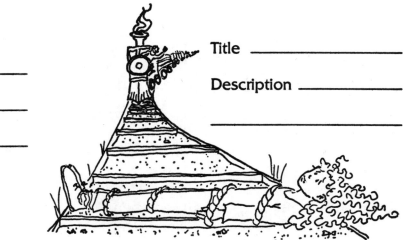

Title _____

Description _____

_____

Title _____

Description _____

_____

Title _____

Description _____

_____

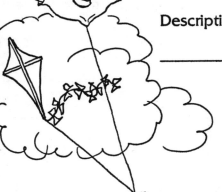

Title _____

Description _____

_____

Title _____

Description _____

_____

SPLIT DECISIONS

Read each problem below and rate the decision made to solve the problem.

Explain your reasons for rating the decision as you did.

Then write a sentence telling what you would have done.

Problem 2
Jonathan was riding his mini-bike when he met an older boy he did not know. The boy told Jonathan that he would pay him $2.00 if he could ride the mini-bike for an hour. Jonathan really wanted the money, and so he decided to rent his bike to the stranger.

Decision rating: Good   Fair   Poor

Reason: _____

_____

My decision: _____

_____

Problem 1
Jennifer was going to be late for school so she decided to ride her new bike. Halfway there she met a friend who asked if she could ride the bike around the block just for fun. After thinking about it, Jennifer agreed.

Decision rating: Good   Fair   Poor

Reason: _____

_____

My decision: _____

_____

Problem 3
Bill had a dental appointment at 4:00. His mother told him that he had to go straight home after school. On his way home, Bill realized that he had forgotten his homework. He knew that if he went back to get it he would be late for his appointment. Bill decided to go home.

Decision rating: Good   Fair   Poor

Reason: _____

_____

My decision: _____

_____

For each traffic sign below, name a person who has "directed" you in that way. Describe the situation and how it made you feel.

Examples:

Situation: You planned to finish your homework but a friend talked you into playing ball instead.

Situation: The teacher told you to finish your math work before beginning your art project.

Name: _____

Situation: _____

_____

Reaction: _____

Name: _____

Situation: _____

_____

Reaction: _____

Name: _____

Situation: _____

_____

Reaction: _____

Name: _____

Situation: _____

_____

Reaction: _____

MEETING PEOPLE

What will you say to each of these people when you meet him or her for the first time?

Remember to say something that will make the person want to get to know you.

(Hint: It's helpful to show that you are interested in the person and in what he or she is doing.)

A teacher in school: _____

_____

_____

A new neighbor: _____

_____

_____

A new classmate: _____

_____

_____

A new friend of your parents: _____

_____

_____

An out-of-town visitor of a friend: _____

_____

_____

Someone your own age from another country: _____

_____

_____

If you had the power to grant special wishes to three people, what would the wishes be?

1. My wish for _____

is _____

_____ .

Reason: _____

_____

2. My wish for _____

is _____

_____ .

Reason: _____

_____

3. My wish for _____

is _____

_____ .

Reason: _____

_____

FEELING GOOD!

List the ways these people make you feel good about who you are and what you do.

My teacher makes me feel good when she/he:

1. _____
2. _____
3. _____

My parents make me feel good when they:

1. _____
2. _____
3. _____

I make myself feel good when I:

1. _____
2. _____
3. _____

My friends make me feel good when they:

1. _____
2. _____
3. _____

List three things you do to make other people feel good.

1. _____
2. _____
3. _____

INTERESTS INVENTORY

Complete this interview sheet by asking people of the given ages
 what interests they have, what hobbies they enjoy, and what skills
 are needed for their hobbies.

Name	Age	Interests	Hobbies	Skills Needed
	5			
	8			
	10			
	12			
	14			
	16			
	18 - 20			
	21 - 30			
	31 - 40			
	41 - 60			

List three interests that you have now that you did not have five years ago.

1. _____ 2. _____ 3. _____

Make a chart to show what you think your interests will be in the future.

GROUP WORK

Choose a word to complete the first sentence for each pair below.
You may use the words on this page or other words of your own choice.
Then complete the second sentence to explain the statement.

entertaining

helpful

outgoing

kind

fair

generous

needy

friendly

1. On my first day at school, my classmates

   were very _____ .

   This made me feel _____ .

2. When I participate in a group, I feel

   _____ .

   I feel this way because _____

   _____ .

3. Groups like me because I am _____

   _____ .

   They like this about me because _____

   _____

   _____ .

4. I like working in a _____

   group.

   I feel this way because _____

   _____

   _____ .

honest

5. My friends are _____ .

   They are this way because _____

   _____ .

6. I feel _____

   when the group excludes me.

   I feel this way because _____

   _____

BELIEFS ON THE LINE

List the things these people in your life *can* do and the things you believe they *could* do if they tried.

PARENTS

I know my parents can:

1. _____

2. _____

I believe my parents could:

1. _____

2. _____

TEACHER

I know my teacher can:

1. _____

2. _____

I believe my teacher could:

1. _____

2. _____

FRIENDS

I know my friends can:

1. _____

2. _____

I believe my friends could:

1. _____

2. _____

OUR CLASS

I know our class can:

1. _____

2. _____

I believe our class could:

1. _____

2. _____

MYSELF

I know I can:

1. _____

2. _____

I believe I could:

1. _____

2. _____

SENSITIVELY SPEAKING

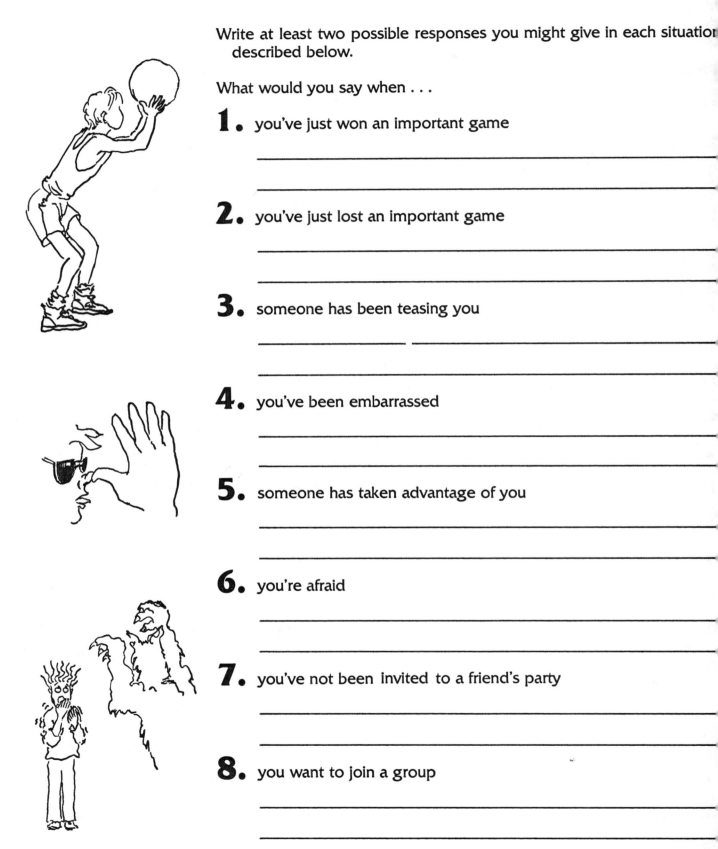

Write at least two possible responses you might give in each situation described below.

What would you say when . . .

1. you've just won an important game

_____

_____

2. you've just lost an important game

_____

_____

3. someone has been teasing you

_____

_____

4. you've been embarrassed

_____

_____

5. someone has taken advantage of you

_____

_____

6. you're afraid

_____

7. you've not been invited to a friend's party

_____

_____

8. you want to join a group

_____

_____

SURVIVAL KIT

Imagine that you are stranded on an island.
You can choose three people and three things to have with you.
Describe the people, their skills, and the things you would want to have
   with you to assure your survival.
Give the reasons for your choices.

People:

1. _____

Skills: _____

Reasons: _____

2. _____

Skills: _____

Reasons: _____

3. _____

Skills: _____

Reasons: _____

Things:

1. _____

Reasons: _____

2. _____

Reasons: _____

3. _____

Reasons: _____

IN FOCUS

Imagine that you can see things the way other people do when you put on their glasses.

Describe each "situation" from your point of view and then from the other person's point of view.

1. Describe yourself as a worker in school from your point of view.

_____

_____

Now put on these glasses and describe yourself as a worker from your teacher's point of view.

_____

_____

2. Describe yourself as a neighbor and friend from your point of view.

_____

_____

Now put on these glasses and describe yourself from your neighbor's point of view.

_____

_____

3. Describe yourself as a family member from your point of view.

_____

_____

Now put on these glasses and describe yourself as a family member from your parents' point of view.

_____

_____

In each "situation," what is the difference between the two points of view?

CLASS DESCRIPTIONS

Describe three of your classmates with "category words" that remind you of the qualities they possess.
Then ask your classmates to guess whom you have described!

Example: Classmate: <u>Peggy</u>
Color descriptor: <u>blue</u> . . . because she is calm
Animal descriptor: <u>turtle</u> . . . because she is slow and steady
Career descriptor: <u>scientist</u> . . . would make a good scientist
Mood descriptor: <u>thoughtful</u> . . . concerned about others
Leisure time descriptor: <u>reading</u> . . . likes to read
Talent or skill descriptor: <u>math</u> . . . skilled mathematician

Classmate #1: _____
Color descriptor: _____
Animal descriptor: _____
Career descriptor: _____
Mood descriptor: _____
Leisure time descriptor: _____
Talent or skill descriptor: _____

Classmate #2: _____
Color descriptor: _____
Animal descriptor: _____
Career descriptor: _____
Mood descriptor: _____
Leisure time descriptor: _____
Talent or skill descriptor: _____

Classmate #3: _____
Color descriptor: _____
Animal descriptor: _____
Career descriptor: _____
Mood descriptor: _____
Leisure time descriptor: _____
Talent or skill descriptor: _____

Now describe yourself using the same formula!

EMERGENCY PRESCRIPTIONS

Read each emergency situation and write a "prescription" that would help the victim. Don't forget to tell where to go for help, whom to see, and what to ask.

Joey was having fun playing tennis when he fell and twisted his arm.

Prescription for Joey:

Prescription for Cindy:

Cindy was having a good time at the party until she ripped her dress.

Jane was on her way to school and realized that she had forgotten an overdue library book.

Prescription for Jane:

Prescription for Mr. Peters:

Mr. Peters, the principal, was on his way to school when he realized that his car was out of gas.

Jennifer has to write a report about dinosaurs, but she doesn't know where to find information on the topic.

Prescription for Jennifer:

TOGETHER SEARCH

Use each of these "together" words in a sentence.
Use a dictionary if you need help.

1. Accomplice: _____

2. Dependent: _____

3. Flock: _____

4. Group: _____

5. Pack: _____

6. Partner: _____

7. Relationship: _____

8. Team: _____

9. Troop: _____

Find the "together" words listed above in this word search puzzle.
Some letters are used more than once.

```
R E L A T I O N S H I P
S M E G E F L O C K Y P A
A N D R A G R O U P O C K
A C C O M P L I C E U K
T R O O P A R T N E R M
A D E P E N D E N T U S
```

Use the clues below and the puzzle letters above to find this
"together" coded message:

1. 2nd space from the top left, 2nd space down: a 2-letter word across
2. 1st space on the top left, 3rd space down: a 3-letter word across
3. 11th space from the top left, 2nd space down: a 3-letter word down
4. 11th space from the top left, 6th space down: a 2-letter word across

___ ___   ___ ___ ___   ___ ___ ___   =   ___ ___

  1   2   3   4   *Answer Key

SKILL CHARTING

List two skills that you have and that you could help someone else to acquire.

Some skills to think about are sports and games, school subjects, dancing, yard work, knitting, building, etc.

1. _____

2. _____

Choose one of the skills above and write the instructions you would give to your "learner."

Write your information on the chart below.

SKILL CHART

Skill:

Materials Needed:

Time Needed:

Number of People Involved:

Directions and Rules:

Describe the qualities you admire in your best friend with words or phrases beginning with the letters below.

R _____

_____

E _____

N _____

D _____

Describe one of your classmates using the letters below.

C _____

L _____

A _____

S _____

S _____

Describe the qualities you admire in your teacher with words or phrases beginning with the letters below.

T _____

E _____

A _____

C _____

H _____

E _____

R _____

Describe yourself using the letters in your first name.

ADMIRATION

Make a list of seven people you admire (friends, historical figures, actors, teachers, inventors, sports stars, etc.).
Write a short description telling what you like best about each person.
Then list skills or qualities you can develop to be more like each person.

People I Admire		
Name	What I Like About This Person	What I Can Do To Be Like This Person

Write the name of a fictional character you admire.
Then write one sentence telling why you admire this character.

_____ (fictional character)

_____

_____

TRUE TRAITS

Check your "true traits"!

Use this key: yes **O**   no **X**   not sure **?**

I . . .

____ have knowledge of the human body
____ have the ability to change a person's mind
____ have the ability to make and keep records
____ have mathematical skills
____ use my hands well
____ express my ideas well
____ listen to other people
____ use good grammar
____ can entertain people
____ can draw or paint
____ can read music
____ spell and write well
____ put things together properly
____ can repair broken things
____ have knowledge of plants
____ have knowledge of animals
____ have knowledge of hand tools
____ have knowledge of machines
____ can sew
____ can type
____ enjoy being with others
____ like science
____ write reports well
____ can win the confidence of others

1. Write the name and a brief job description of an occupation you might like to have when you become a part of the working world.

_____

_____

2. List the natural abilities needed for success in this occupation.

_____

_____

3. Do your "true traits" match the job description and the abilities needed for this occupation?

_____

© 1989 by Incentive Publications, Inc., Nashville, TN.

69

GOALS GALORE

Look up the definition for the word "goal" in the dictionary.
Write the definition in your own words.

Goal: _____

Write a personal goal for today. _____

_____

List the things you will have to do to reach this goal.

1. _____

2. _____

3. _____

If you complete these tasks, you should be able to meet your goal by the end of the day!

Think about yesterday.
Write a goal that you met yesterday.

_____

Write a goal that you should have met yesterday but didn't.

_____

What could you have done to meet this goal?

_____

_____

Write a goal for tomorrow.

_____

Write a goal for the week.

_____

Write a personal goal that can be met by the end of the year.

_____

List three things you must do to reach this goal.

1. _____

2. _____

3. _____

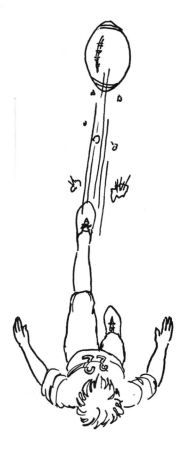

After setting a goal, the next step is to plan how to achieve the goal.
Practice your planning skills by completing these "ladders to success."

Select two goals you want to accomplish — one for school and one for home.
Start at the bottom of the ladder and list the steps you will need to take to reach the goal.

Goal:

5.

4.

3.

2.

1.

Goal:

5.

4.

3.

2.

1.

LEARNING UNLIMITED

Answer these questions about what you have learned and what you want to learn in the future.

1. What new thing did you learn today? _____

_____

Who taught it to you? _____

2. What did you learn *more* about today? _____

_____

Who taught it to you? _____

3. What question would you like to have answered? _____

_____

To what person or place could you go to find the answer to this question?

_____

4. What new skill would you like to learn in the next month? _____

_____

Who can teach you this skill? _____

5. What would you like to learn next year? _____

_____

Where can you learn it? _____

Who can teach it to you? _____

6. What skill can you teach someone else? _____

TURN-A-BOUTS

Turn a hobby into a career.
List the things you like to do in your free time.
What career could you make out of each interest?
Write the possibilities in the space provided.

Things I Like To Do In My Free Time	A Possible Career
1. _____	1. _____
2. _____	2. _____
3. _____	3. _____
4. _____	4. _____
5. _____	5. _____
6. _____	6. _____
7. _____	7. _____
8. _____	8. _____
9. _____	9. _____
10. _____	10. _____

IF THE SHOE FITS . . .

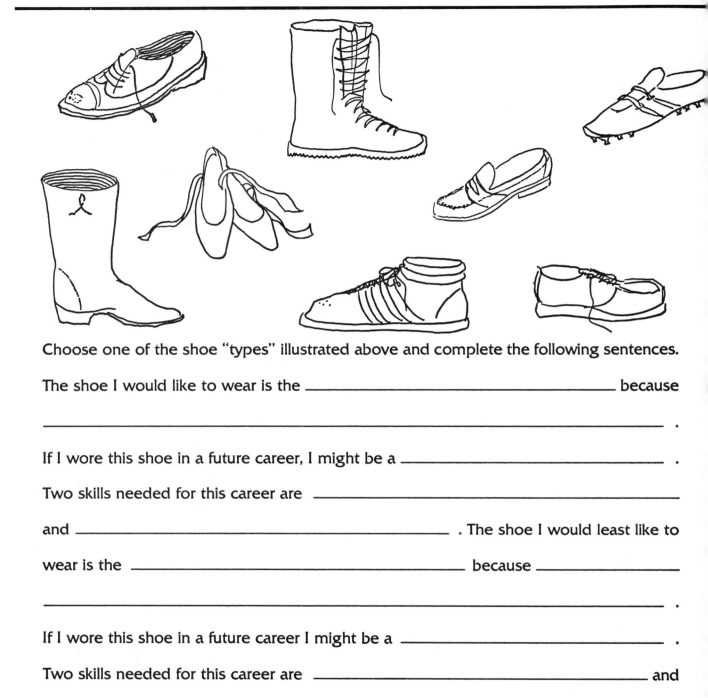

Choose one of the shoe "types" illustrated above and complete the following sentences.

The shoe I would like to wear is the _____ because

_____ .

If I wore this shoe in a future career, I might be a _____ .

Two skills needed for this career are _____

and _____ . The shoe I would least like to

wear is the _____ because _____

_____ .

If I wore this shoe in a future career I might be a _____ .

Two skills needed for this career are _____ and

_____ .

Draw another type of shoe that you would like to wear in the future.

FILLING THE WORK BILL

1. List the traits that can lead to success on the invoice on the right.
List the traits that can lead to failure on the invoice on the left.

2. Check the success traits you have with a red crayon.
Check the failure traits you have with a green crayon.

3. Record the number of checks on each invoice.

4. Write three sentences telling how you might improve your "work bill."

_____

_____

_____

tardy	careless	polite
hard working	regular attendance	rude
punctual	abusive of equipment	wasteful
thrifty	lazy	independent
alert	inattentive	inconsistent

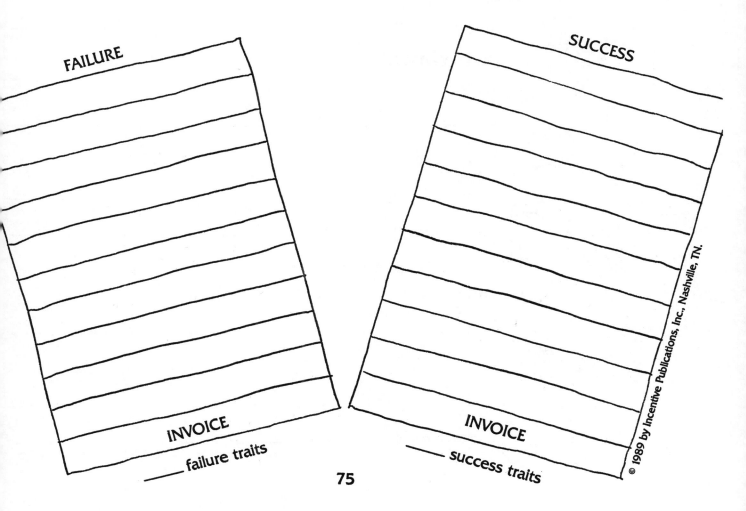

FAILURE

INVOICE

_____ failure traits

SUCCESS

INVOICE

_____ success traits

SKILL SCAN

Complete this skill inventory by listing your present skills, your future skill goals, and the things you need to do to reach your goals.

Topic: SPORTS
Present skills:

I am able to _____

Future Goal:

I want to be able to _____

To reach my goal I must _____

Topic: SCHOOLWORK
Present skills:

I am able to _____

Future Goal:

I want to be able to _____

To reach my goal I must _____

Topic: BEHAVIOR
Present skills:

I am able to _____

Future Goal:

I want to be able to _____

To reach my goal I must _____

Topic: HUMAN RELATIONSHIPS
Present skills:

I am able to _____

Future Goal:

I want to be able to _____

To reach my goal I must _____

PHOTO ALBUM

Imagine what your life might be like when you are 29 years old.
Answer these questions and "illustrate" the photo album.

My job in 20 _____

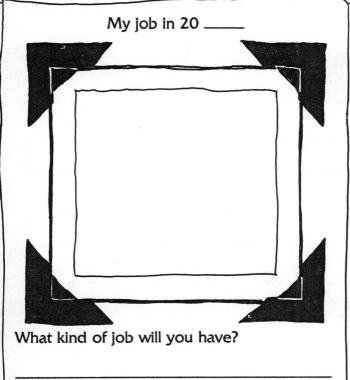

What kind of job will you have?

_____

My home in 20 _____

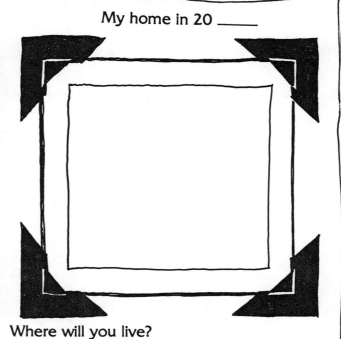

Where will you live?

_____

My car in 20 _____

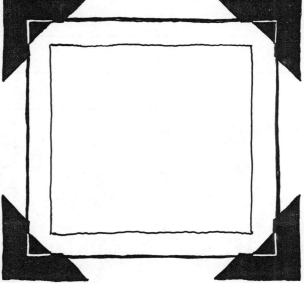

What kind of car will you own?

_____

Me and my family in 20 _____

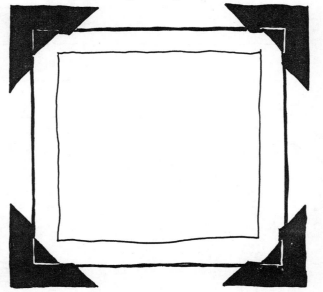

How many people will there be in your family?

_____

TIME CAPSULE

Imagine that you could live in any time — past, present, or future.
Write a story about the time in which you would most like to live.
Include an imaginary description of yourself, the people you would know, the things you
   would do, and the way you would feel.

_____

_____

_____

_____

_____

_____

_____

_____

_____

_____

_____

_____

_____

_____

Page 21:

Page 23:

Page 28:

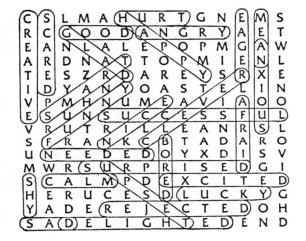

Page 65:

Coded Message: Me and you = us